Words for Auction
A Guide to Acronyms and Jargon
Commonly Used on eBay

By Danna Crawford
and "Uncle Joe" Adamson

ISBN 978-0-6152-1558-7

This book is dedicated to our ridiculously supportive spouses, James and Cindy, who put up with the phone calls and the meetings and the boxes and the bubblewrap and the general *mostly*-organized insanity that comes along with getting bitten by the eBay bug.

ฉฉฉ

We'd like to express our appreciation to all of our friends in the eBay community that have supported our efforts to help others, particularly Jim, Kathie, Rob, Mel, Cheryl, Jon and Carla. Special thanks to our friends in the Voices of the Community, EdSpecs and Mentors programs who prove every day that community spirit overcomes tumultuous change.

"Uncle Joe" Adamson

The terms and language used on eBay have grown rapidly over the years. As the site has evolved, new concepts and policies have been introduced. Meanwhile, my memory and my eyesight have gone the wrong direction! I wasn't sure I could keep up with it all at times.

Recently, I began working with a new group of people completely unfamiliar with many of these acronyms, terms and concepts that I'm used to seeing on eBay. It was tough for me to remember to make sense of it all while teaching these new eBayers. I started jotting down all the different things they had questions about to make a useful list of jargon.

Soon after, I ran into Danna, who also had an interest in putting together a sort of eBay Dictionary. She too was working with folks that needed some kind of primer or reference to make understanding eBay lingo a little easier. The result of our collaboration is this book, the first, I hope, of more to come.

It's a real joy to me to be able to bring information and education to you, our friends in the eBay community. I hope this helps you have a great time, make new friends and enjoy a profitable eBay experience.

"Uncle Joe" Adamson
Oklahoma City, OK

<u>A Note from the Author</u>
Danna Crawford

As an active member of the eBay community I was inspired by Ruth, a fellow eBayer I met in August 2007. She presented a few questions to my peers and thanks to her, my brainstorming had begun: We needed a reference book to decode all these crazy things we say and talk about every day on eBay!

I'm especially thankful to another eBay member that came into my life: Uncle Joe! I feel this man is a true godsend as we both share not only the love of writing, but the love of helping others be the best eBay users they can be!

This is the first reference book we've done. If you like it, please let us know because there's plenty more we could cover for you.

By keeping this book in a convenient place by your computer you'll finally be able to understand those funny phrases fellow eBayer's are using.

I'm looking forward to hearing from all of you in eBay Land!

Danna Crawford
Ocala, FL

Using the Reference Guide

New and experienced eBay visitors run into all sorts of acronyms, terms, slang and concepts every day. There are far more in use than appear here in this little book! We've tried to give you a good mix of the most common, though, with a few interesting ones added in to spice things up.

You should be careful adding acronyms to your own listing titles and descriptions until you're very sure they'll be helpful. There is a larger audience on the internet than ever before, and those people come to eBay *not knowing* the acronyms you might be using. These descriptive acronyms were created because of space limitations in item titles. "MIMP" takes much less room than "Mint In Mint Package", but potential buyers may not know to look for that – or understand it if they see it.

The items that follow are divided into three groups:

- Items marked as *conversational* are generally used in chats and messages.

- Items marked as *descriptive* are generally used in listing titles or descriptions.

- The remaining items are general terms and concepts.

Words for Auction
A Guide to Acronyms and Jargon
Commonly Used on eBay

0-9

~~~ conversational

Waves, as in "I'm waving hello."

^^^ conversational

We're on the same wavelength

((hugs)) *conversational*
Surrounding a name with parenthesis denotes Hugs

30 Day Rule

Federal Trade Commission (FTC) provision, the "Mail or Telephone Order Merchandise Rule," that specifies a 30 day time limit on the shipment of goods, order cancellation, refunds, and some credit card issues.

3P

Third Party, 3rd Party. An outside person or company providing a service or product.

501(c)3

Non-Profit Organization (NPO). Derived from the reference location in the Tax Code.

A

AAMOF *conversational*
As A Matter Of Fact

AB
See Announcement Boards

Danna Crawford & Uncle Joe Adamson

About Me

A page provided to each eBay member for their personal use.

Accounting Assistant

A free program that helps integrate eBay and PayPal with QuickBooks.

ACEO *descriptive*

Art Cards, Editions and Originals. These are small works of art, about the size of a playing card, always 3.5" x 2.5".

Acceptance

The point at which an item is received by the USPS or other shipping service.

Addy *conversational*

Address

AFAIC *conversational*

As Far As I'm Concerned

AFAICT *conversational*

As Far As I Can Tell

AFAIK *conversational*

As Far As I Know

Affiliate Program

A program that allows other people or companies to market another company's goods and services for a commission.

AFK *conversational*

Away From Keyboard

AKA *conversational*

Also Known As

AMEX

American Express credit card

Analytics

Usually referring to measurements (metrics) of website activity used to gauge site traffic, click-through performance, etc.

Announcement Boards

AB. Found in the Community section, these pages offer news, information and events from eBay.

Answer Center

A community-supported area for questions about eBay topics.

As Is *descriptive*

Item offered in its present condition, with no return offered.

As Is Where Is *descriptive*

Item is offered in its present condition and location, with no return offered. Buyer is expected to pick up or arrange transportation/shipping.

ASP

Average Sales Price. The median value of an item in the market.

ASQ

Ask Seller a Question. Member email related to an item sent via eBay.

ATC *descriptive*

Art Trading Cards

Auction

Items listed on eBay that allow for competitive bidding, with the highest bidder winning at a set completion time.

Auction Bytes

Website focusing on the happenings of online auction sites.

Auctiva

A popular company offering services to eBay sellers.

AUD

Australian Dollar, the currency of Australia.

AUTH *descriptive*

Authentic

Avatar

Graphic used to represent a person (or personality).

Average Sales Price

ASP. Median value of an item in the market.

B

B&M

Brick and Mortar. A physical store.

B&W *descriptive*

Black & White

B2B

Business to Business.

B2C

Business to Consumer, Business to Customer

BAK *conversational*

Back At Keyboard

BBL

Blocked Bidder List. List of member names you block to prevent bids or purchases.

BC *descriptive*
Back Cover

Best Offer

A feature that allows a buyer to make a price offer to a seller. The seller can accept, decline or make a counter-offer.

Best Match

A search option that uses several criteria to produce a "best selection" of available items eBay believes will match the intent of the search.

Best Practices

The methods, processes and practices that reliably produce desirable results.

Bidder

A person placing bids in an effort to win an auction item.

BIN

Buy It Now. An immediate purchase.

BISBE *conversational*

Butt In Seat, Brain Engaged

Blackthorne

A seller's tool offered by subscription.

Blocked Bidder List

BBL. List of member names you block from bidding or purchasing.

Blog

Self-published serial internet content, often a cross between a journal, newspaper column and a soapbox.

BO

Best Offer. Feature that allows Buyer to make a counter-offer to Seller's asking price.

Boardies *conversational*

Slang for people that participate on Discussion Boards.

Bobal

Popular iconic boardie often found assisting the community in Discussion Boards.

BOGO *descriptive*

Buy One Get One

BOHO *descriptive*

Bohemian, a modern stylized hippie look.

Bottom Line

Net Income. Revenue less costs and expenses.

BPP *also* **PBP**

See Buyer Protection Policy

BRB *conversational*

Be Right Back

Brokerage Fees

Fees charged by shippers like UPS or FedEx to move parcels through international Customs.

Buyer

A person that has ordered/purchased an item offered for sale.

Buyer Protection

BPP *or* PBP. Paypal program that offers qualified protection to Buyers with INR or SNAD claims.

C

CAPTCHA

"Completely Automated Public Turing test to tell Computers and Humans Apart". A graphic challenge shown with a series of malformed, warped or obscured letters, numbers or words meant to distinguish between people activity and computer attacks.

Carp *conversational*

Euphemism for the obscene word.

Cash Flow

The money taken in and spent in a given time period.

Category

The various groups into which items are divided by product type.

CBT

Cross-Border Trade. International Sales.

CEM

Contact eBay Member. General messages sent to member, not otherwise ASQ/RTQ.

Chargeback

A disputed payment on a credit card resulting in the payment being reversed.

Chat

A conversation conducted online in real time. A chat may be between two or more people.

Chatter

The official eBay newsletter, presented in Blog form.

Churn

Acquisition and loss of a measured group by time or percentage. Short for "churn rate."

Classified Ad

A type of listing that advertises a product or service, but is not sold on eBay.

Click-Through-Rate

CTR. Measurement of the success of Pay-per-Click (PPC) ads.

COA *descriptive*

Certificate of Authenticity

COGS

Cost of Goods Sold, or Cost of Sales. This is the cost of the manufacture and assembly of product. COGS is subtracted from Revenue to calculate Gross Margin.

Combined Shipping

Adding multiple purchases together as a single order to provide the most economical shipping cost.

Community

The buyers and sellers on eBay that support and entertain each other through discussion boards, chats, groups, blogs, reviews and guides and other means.

Community Values

The foundational philosophy of eBay, that "People are basically good; Everyone has something to contribute; An honest, open environment brings out the best in people; eBay recognizes and respects everyone as unique individuals; eBay encourages members to treat each other as they'd want to be treated."

Completed Listing

Items that have been offered on eBay and finished are said to be *completed*.

Conversion Rate

CR. Measurable number of desired or successful actions taken, usually sales-related, but broader in context. Examples: number of sales from a group of listings; members that click to join a newsletter; visitors to your store that result in sales.

Core

Term for eBay's primary search of Auction or Fixed Price listings.

Counter

A number, usually shown as a graphic, that represents the number of times a webpage has been visited.

CR

Conversion Rate. Measurable number of desired or successful actions taken, usually sales-related, but broader in context. Examples: number of sales from a group of listings; members that click to join a newsletter; visitors to your store that result in sales.

Cross-Border Trade

CBT. International Sales.

CSR

Customer Service Representative

CTR

Click-Through-Rate. Measurement of the success of Pay-Per-Click (PPC) ads.

D

Dashboard

See Seller Dashboard

DB

Discussion Board. A place that combines messages into various categories for topical discussion.

DB *descriptive*

Double-breasted, found in clothing

DC *descriptive*

Dust Cover

DC

Delivery Confirmation

Delivery Confirmation

DC. USPS service that confirms the date and time a mailed item was delivered. [This is often mistaken for package *tracking*. It's not the same.]

Detailed Seller Ratings

DSRs. Feedback 2.0 rating stars.

DHL

DHL parcel service

Discussion Board

DB. A place that combines messages into various categories for topical discussion.

Dispute Console

A function from *My eBay* that helps manage disputes between buyers and sellers during a trade.

Dispute Resolution

Processes in place to facilitate communication between Buyer and Seller; sometimes involving eBay, Paypal or both depending on the situation. Disputes are generally: Non-performing Seller (NPS), Item Not Received (INR), Significantly Not As Described (SNAD), or Unpaid Item (UI).

DJ *descriptive*

Dust Jacket

DMCA

Digital Millennium Copyright Act. Federal law that requires an internet service to remove material that is claimed to infringe on a copyright owner's rights. eBay's VeRO program assists with these claims.

DOA *descriptive*
Dead on Arrival. Describes a product that doesn't work when delivered.

DOUA

Disabled Online Users Association. Group providing education, resources and support to disabled internet users.

DSRs

Detailed Seller Ratings. Feedback 2.0 rating stars.

Dutch Auction

An auction format that is little-used due to its complexity. Multiple items are offered, with multiple winners competing for different quantities at a final price set by the lowest successful bidder.

E

EAPG *descriptive*

Early American Pattern Glass

eBay Live!

A combination convention/trade show offering eBay members a chance to network, attend educational classes, discover new products and services, and meet eBay employees and executives.

eBay Motors

Specialty site focusing on the sale of vehicles, parts and accessories.

eBay Time

On eBay.com, the official time used is that of eBay HQ in San Jose, CA – Pacific Time. The official eBay time can usually be found as a link at the bottom of their web pages.

eBay Toolbar

Product that offers improved security and convenient bidding.

eCommerce

Business conducted on the internet.

ECMTA

E-Commerce Merchants Trade Association. Trade association of small- and medium-size eCommerce businesses. Partnered with *PeSA*.

e/DC

Electronic Delivery Confirmation. A barcode printed on USPS mailing labels used for scanning at delivery.

EdSpec

See Education Specialist.

Education Specialist

ES. EdSpec. Person licensed to teach official eBay University curriculum via the Education Specialist program.

EMO *descriptive*

Modern stylized Indie hipster look.

Emoticons *conversational*

Also called *Smileys*. These are text symbols representing a smiling face, or a big laugh, or a tearful pout turned sideways. Messages and chats will often display these as little graphics. Because emotion is not displayed in text, the chief use is to provide a clue about the context in which a remark is made, or the mood that should be understood.

EOD

End of Day

ES

See Education Specialist

Escrow

A service that receives and holds buyer's payment while seller delivers product. Upon buyer's acceptance, payment is released to the seller. [Fake escrow is often used by crooks to build trust with their victims. Be very careful with escrow.]

ESPP

Extended Seller Protection Program. A service offered by PayPal to eBay Sellers to help manage risk.

EST
Eastern Standard Time

EUC *descriptive*
Excellent Used Condition

EULA

End User License Agreement. Usually found with software, a EULA covers the rights agreed to as a condition of use.

EUR

Euros. Currency of European Union member countries.

EXP *descriptive*

Expired

F

FAIC *conversational*

For All I Care

FAIK *conversational*

For All I Know

FAQ

Frequently Asked Questions. A list of common questions with the usual answer provided.

FB

See Feedback

FC *descriptive*
Fine Condition

FedEx *or* FEX

Federal Express parcel service.

Feedback

System of comments and Detailed Seller Rating (DSRs) "stars" left following a trade.

Feedback 2.0

Evolution of feedback from two-way feedback (FB 1.0) to current method that restricts Sellers to positive only feedback for Buyers; Buyers remain free to leave any feedback as desired.

Feedback Extortion

Using the threat of bad feedback to coerce an action or value from a trading partner, usually free product, partial refunds or other consideration. This is an actionable offense of eBay policy.

Feedback Scorecard

A box displaying 30 Day, 6 Month & 12 Month feedback activity

Feedback Star
Seen next to feedback score numbers, a colored star generally represents the number of feedback a member has received.

FIFO

First In, First Out. Inventory method where the first product produced or received sets the value of the SKU. Also used to describe rotation or use of inventory items.

File Exchange

A bulk listing service provided by eBay.

Final Value Fee

FVF. The commission paid to eBay upon a successful sale.

Finding

Synonymous with Search. Finding 2.0 refers specifically to eBay's overhaul of Search to incorporate Relevancy, DSR weighting, and improved speed and accuracy tuning.

Firefox

Popular internet browser program, used to display web pages.

Fixed Price

Type of listing where the item is offered at a set price. Often used when multiple items are available.

Flow

The progression of a series of events; workflow; movement through a form or procedure.

FOB (location)

Freight On Board. The point from which something is to be shipped, usually seen with heavy items.

FP

Fixed Price listings. Listings in core with a set price.

FS *descriptive*
Full Screen. The format size of a DVD's picture.

FVF

Final Value Fee. The commission paid to eBay upon a successful sale.

FVFC

Final Value Fee Credit

G

G *descriptive*

Good. Usually grade or condition.

GAAP

"Generally Accepted Accounting Principles". Standardized rules for accounting.

GBP

Great Britian Pounds. The currency of the UK.

GC *descriptive*

Good Condition

Gently Used *descriptive*

Euphemism of "Like New" for a used item that shows very little wear, if any.

GIF

An image format preferred for its ability to display simple animation or photographic images, particularly where it will appear transparent in combination with other website graphics. Uses the file extension: .gif

Gift Services

Add-on feature that allows gift cards, wrap or special shipping to be offered to buyers with their purchase.

Giving Works

eBay program for non-profit contributions made through sales.

Green

Trend espousing environmental awareness across several areas. Anything promoting decreased environmental impact, alternative energy, recycling, or organic product is considered "Green".

Griff

Jim "Griff" Griffith. Popular eBay company faceman and personality, author and internet radio host covering eBay topics.

Gross Receipts

NPO term synonymous with Top Line or Revenue. The income received by the NPO.

Groups

Discussion boards that are created, maintained and used by the Community for their own special interests.

GTG *or* G2G *conversational*

Got to go, also Good to go

GU *descriptive*
Gently Used. Used item that shows very little wear, if any.

Guides

Articles written by Community members on a variety of topics.

Guides & Reviews

See Guides

H

Hall of Fame *or* **HoF**

Members singled out for recognition by eBay for their contributions and service to the Community.

Half.com

Website specializing in the sale of books and media, owned by eBay.

HB *descriptive*

Hard Back

HBDC *or* **HBDJ**

Hard Back with Dust Cover/Jacket

Hit Counter

A number, usually shown as a graphic, that represents the number of times a webpage has been visited.

Hits

The number of visits a webpage has received.

HM *descriptive*

Hand-made

Host *or* **Hosting**

Information stored on the internet for retrieval resides on a computer or service, called the *Host*. Companies that house websites or other info are *Hosting Services*.

Home Page *or* **HP**
The first or main page of a web site.

HQ

Headquarters. eBay's HQ is in San Jose, CA.

HTF *descriptive*
Hard to Find.

HTML

Hypertext Markup Language. The special markings and language that describes the appearance of a web page. Browser programs understand HTML, interpret it, and turn it into the web pages you see on the internet.

I

IANAL *conversational*

I Am Not A Lawyer

Identity Theft

The act of acquiring or using someone else's credit or personal information in order to commit crime.

ID Verify

A service that verifies personal information to assure identity. Members that have used the service have an identifying graphic beside their member name.

IE

Internet Explorer. Microsoft Windows web browser, used to view web pages.

IM

Instant Message. A message sent directly to another person's computer or cell phone. Some popular programs that provide IM functions are Skype, AIM, Jabber, Google, Yahoo and MSN.

IMA

Internet Merchants Association. A non-profit trade association for companies involved in internet commerce.

IMHO *conversational*

In My Humble Opinion

IMNSHO *conversational*

In My Not So Humble Opinion

IMO *conversational*

In My Opinion

INR

Item Not Received. Buyer claims the item has not arrived.

Instant Message

IM. A message sent directly to another person's computer or cell phone. Some popular programs that provide IM functions are Skype, AIM, Jabber, Google, Yahoo and MSN.

Insurance

Guarantee that covers the value of a shipment in the event of loss, theft or damage. Items improperly packaged are often denied insurance reimbursement. [Some Sellers may attempt to disclaim liability for shipping loss or damage if insurance is not purchased, but US consumer protection laws do not generally support this practice.]

Internet Explorer

IE. Microsoft Windows web browser, used to view web pages.

Interstitial

A page, message, ad, etc. that is inserted strategically to interrupt or create a pause in website event flow.

IS

See Item Specifics.

ISP

Internet Service Provider. A company that provides connection to the internet or other internet services.

Item Not Received

INR. Buyer claims the item has not arrived.

Item Specifics

IS. Nuggets of specific information about a product that can be identified readily by Search. Examples would include size, color, brand, artist, age, material, ISBN, UPC, etc.

J – K

J/K *conversational*

Just Kidding

JPG ("Jay-peg")
A compressed image, preferred for its combination of clarity, small size and faster transmission speeds via internet. Uses the file extension: .jpg

Kijiji

Free classified ads service owned by eBay.

KMA *or* **KMB** *conversational*

Kiss my (rear)

L

L8R *conversational*

Later. Goodbye.

LE *descriptive*

Limited Edition

LIFO

Last In, First Out. Inventory method where the last product produced or received sets the value of the SKU. Also used to describe rotation or use of inventory items.

Listing

An advertisement for an item placed on eBay.

LiveWorld

Vendor that provides social networking services to eBay - chat, db, groups, etc.

LMK *conversational*

Let Me Know

LN *descriptive*

Like New

LOL *conversational*
Laugh Out Loud

LTBX *descriptive*

Letterbox. Describes the widescreen appearance of a video formatted to a regular screen.

LTD *descriptive*

Limited edition

LTS

Live To System. For example, feedback changes went LTS in Februrary 2008.

Lurk *or* **Lurker** *conversational*

Reading discussion boards or chat conversations without actively participating.

M

M2M

Member to member

Mail or Telephone Order Merchandise Rule

30 Day Rule. Federal Trade Commission (FTC) provision that specifies a time limit on the shipment of goods, order cancellation, refunds, and some credit card issues.

Marketplace Research

Subscription service providing research into eBay's past listing data.

Mentors

An extension of the defunct eBay Volunteers program, where active volunteers operate special Community Groups to assist members in a more personalized environment than the public discussion boards.

ME page

A personal webpage provided to each eBay member.

MIB *descriptive*

Mint In Box. Item inside box is in perfect condition.

MIJ *descriptive*

Made In Japan

MIMB *or* **MIMP** *descriptive*

Mint In Mint Box / Package. Both item and box are in perfect condition.

Mint *descriptive*

Absolutely perfect condition. Also abbreviated MNT. [Skepticism is healthy with claims of "mint condition."]

MIP *descriptive*

Mint In Package. Item is in perfect condition, in package.

Mission Fish

Administers eBay's Giving Works program for non-profit contributions made through sales.

M/m

Month over Month. Comparison of performance.

MNB *descriptive*

Mint No Box. Perfect item, but no box.

MOC *descriptive*

Mint On Card. Item is in perfect condition, on display card.

MOMC *descriptive*

Mint On Mint Card. Item is in perfect condition on a display card, also in perfect condition.

Month over Month

M/m. Comparison of performance.

MOS

Multi-Order Shipping. A PayPal service allowing many orders to be shipped by creating mailing labels in a batch.

MP3

An audio recording with the file extension MP3. Popular format used to store music, as the compressed file is quite small while retaining good quality.

MWMT *descriptive*

Mint With Mint Tags. Item is in perfect conditions, with perfect tags.

My eBay

Central control panel for a member's buying and selling activity. Found on the top menu selection.

N

NARU (Nay-roo)

Not A Registered User. A suspended or closed eBay account.

NBW *descriptive*

Never Been Worn

NC *descriptive*

No Cover

Near Mint *descriptive*

Item is in nearly perfect condition. Abbreviated as NM, NMINT, NRMT.

NEG

Negative feedback

Negative

Negative feedback score or comment.

Net Income

Bottom Line. Profit. Revenue less costs and expenses.

NEUT *conversational*

Neutral feedback

Neutral

Neutral feedback score or comment.

Newbies *conversational*

Slang for new users.

NIB *descriptive*

New In Box. Item is in new condition, in original packaging.

Niche ("Nich")

A specialty.

NLA *descriptive*

No Longer Available

NM *or* **NMINT** *descriptive*

Near Mint. Item is in nearly perfect condition.

NOS *descriptive*

New Old Stock. Item is in new packaged condition, but the item may be aged.

NR *descriptive*

No Reserve. An item offered for auction without a hidden minimum sales price.

NRFB *descriptive*

Never Removed From Box

NRFP *descriptive*

Never Removed From Package

NRMT *descriptive*

Near Mint

NUT *conversational*

Neutral feedback. Also NEUT.

NWOT *descriptive*

New Without Tags

NWT *descriptive*

New With Tags

O

OEM *descriptive*

Original Equipment Manufacturer

OOAK *descriptive*

One of a Kind

OOP *descriptive*

Out Of Print

OP *conversational*

Original Post or Poster. The first message in a discussion thread or its author are both OP.

OTOH *conversational*

On the other hand

Outbid

The result of any new bid on an auction that is higher than the previous bid.

Oz

Ounce

P

Partial Refund

Return of a portion of a payment, usually due to a postage overcharge or an adjustment to the value of an item.

PayPay *conversational*
Euphemism for PayPal

Pay-per-Click

PPC. Outside or 3rd Party ads that pay the host when a browsing person clicks the ad.

PBP

See Paypal Buyer Protextion

Peeps *conversational*

Slang for People

PeSA

Professional eBay Sellers Alliance. Trade association dedicated to eBay selling professionals.

Pharming

An attempt to steal personal information through false websites. Example: Website that looks like Paypal or a fake escrow company. Often combined with phishing.

Phishing

An attempt to steal personal information through social engineering. Example: Phoney notice of account closure that asks for updated personal information.

Photobucket

A popular website offering picture hosting.

PICNIC *conversational*

Problem in chair not in computer

Picture Manager

A subscription picture hosting service offered by eBay.

Pink

eBay employees. When posting on discussion boards, their message headers are pink.

Pink-slap *conversational*

Slang for getting an official moderation warning or suspension while in eBay chat or discussion boards. Euphemisms like "taking a cruise" or "voted off the island" or being on a "vacation" are often used for those suspended, as they seem to vanish.

Pink's Lounge

Designated gathering place at *eBay Live!* convention floor where eBay employees and management mingle casually with attendees.

PM

Priority Mail

Podcast

An audio recording published for access over the internet for PC playback or download to a portable audio device like an iPod or other MP3 player.

POS *or* POSI *conversational*

Positive feedback

POS

Point of Sale. Where a sale is made.

Positive

Positive feedback score or comment

PowerSeller

PS. Sellers meeting certain criteria are eligible for eBay's PowerSeller program. PowerSellers have access to additional message boards, services, customer service and promotion.

PP

PayPal. Payment service owned by eBay.

PPC

Pay-per-click. Outside or 3rd Party ads that pay the host when a browsing person clicks the ad.

Preferences

An area of *My eBay* that allows some system settings to be configured.

Profit

Bottom Line. Net Income. Revenue less costs and expenses.

Prolly *conversational*

Probably

Proof of Delivery

Verification that a shipment has been delivered.

Proof of Shipment

Verification that a shipment has been made.

ProStores

An eCommerce web hosting service owned by eBay.

Proxy Bid

A bid placed that is higher than required to reach the next successful bid increment. Any new bids received are automatically bid against by the computer until the item is won or the proxy bid amount has been exhausted.

PS

See PowerSeller

PST

Pacific Standard Time

Push-back

Resistance to policy change or economic forces. eBay has gained notoriety over attempts to induce user or market behaviors, the cumulative effect being strong push-back from the affected community at any change.

Q

Q&A

Questions & Answers

QA

Quality Assurance. The practice of monitoring production quality.

QTY

Quantity

R

Relevancy

Term describing the relation between two linked sites or other content items. The more related, the greater the relevancy. In the broader context, the more things are alike or have to do with each other, the better the quality of a search return. This concept of relevancy is the basis for processes like "Best Match."

Reseller Marketplace

Specialized area offering B2B bulk sales to eBay PowerSellers.

Reserve

A hidden minimum sales price used in conjunction with an auction.

Resolution Center

Area on PayPal that manages communications and progress during trading disputes.

Reviews & Guides

Area of eBay containing product reviews and articles written by community members.

Revise

The ability to change or update an active item listing.

RET

Retired. A style or product that has been discontinued.

Retaliatory Feedback

Feedback left to punish a trading partner, usually for leaving a neutral or negative. Retaliatory Feedback is cited as the chief reason for Feedback 2.0.

Revenue

Top Line. The income received from the sale of goods and service. NPOs use "Gross Receipts".

River, the *conversational*

Euphemism for Amazon.com

Roll-Out

Process of taking a product Live To System (LTS). This is often a bumpy process, as system complexity always creates unforeseen issues.

ROTFL *conversational*

Rolling on the Floor Laughing

ROTFLMAO *or* ROTFLMBO *conversational*

Rolling on the Floor, Laughing My [rear] Off

RSVP *conversational*

Please respond. Usually to confirm attendance or participation.

RTM *conversational*

Read the manual

RTQ

Reply to Question. Message response to an ASQ.

S

SAHD

Stay At Home Dad

SAHM

Stay At Home Mom

SB *descriptive*

Single Breasted, found in clothing

Sales Reports

Service provided by eBay that offers basic graphs and sales performance measurement.

SCAN

USPS service that combines electronic Delivery Confirmation (e/DC) barcodes onto a single form for ease of processing. The resulting form generates an *Acceptance* of all the referenced items being shipped with a single laser scan.

SCO

See Second Chance Offer

SCR *descriptive*

Scratch

SE *descriptive*

Special Edition

Second Chance Offer

SCO. An offer made to unsuccessful bidders in an auction to purchase the item at their final bid. Often used by sellers with additional quantity of an item, or when the winning bidder fails to complete the purchase.

Seller Account

Area of *My eBay* that reports sales activity, service and subscription fees and credits.

Seller Central

Area offering tips and resources of interest to eBay sellers.

Seller Dashboard

Central display of various measurements of a seller's performance.

Seller Protection Policy

SPP. A Paypal program that offers qualified protection to Sellers meeting certain criteria against loss from credit card chargebacks or reversals.

Selling Manager

A subscription tool that automates many routine Seller functions.

Sell-through Rate

STR. The percent sold of product in a given time frame.

SEO

Search Engine Optimization. The practice of adjusting website content to improve Search Engine rankings.

S&H

Shipping and Handling. The amount of postage or shipping plus costs of materials and packing resources to make a parcel ready for transit.

Shill Bidding

Forbidden practice of bidding on one's own auction listing to artificially drive up the price.

Shipping Calculator

A listing function that determine postage or shipping cost.

Shipping Center

Area of eBay offering information and resources for shipping.

Shipscript

Popular member providing free tools for eBay sellers. 2007 Community Hall of Fame award recipient.

SIC

Stores in Core, synonymous with SIS - Stores In Search.

SIF

Store Inventory Format. Listings that are specific to eBay Stores.

SIG *descriptive*

See Signature.

Siggy *conversational*

Sig. *See* Signature

Signature

Personalized graphics and text appended to the bottom of messages.

SIS

Stores in Search. The appearance of Stores items (SIF) in core. Notorious eBay reversal event where SIS produced dramatic sales increases, but eBay quickly removed with a number of confused statements that often appeared contradictory. Continues to play a major role in Seller push-back today.

Site Map

A central area showing the main structure of a website.

SKU ("skyew" or "S-K-U")

Stock Keeping Unit is a uniquely identified product (not quantity) or style. A trading card seller may have sets of Pokeman Silver and Magic the Gathering, two SKUs. A vending machine with 12 unique product choices holds 12 SKUs. This is meaningful in the context of Stores (SIF) or Fixed Price (FP) listings, where a Seller may have thousands of SKUs.

Skype

Instant Message, voice chat and telephone-over-internet service owned by eBay.

SMI

Safeguarding Member IDs. Replacement of member names with random characters to protect identity. For example, unclejoeadamson might appear in a listing's bid activity as m***s.

Smileys *conversational*

See Emoticons

SMS

Short Message Service. Text messages sent to a cell phone.

SNAD

Significantly Not As Described. The item varies from the description given in a substantial way.

Snipe *or* **Sniping**

Bidding in the final moments of an auction in an attempt to get the lowest possible price while preventing a reaction from competitors.

Sniper

Someone who *Snipes.*

S/O *descriptive*

Sold Out

Social Networking

Web 2.0. The interaction between people with similar interests or activities producing content,collaboration and communications within distinct online communities. Chat, discussion boards, Reviews & Guides, Blogs, My World, Groups, ME pages are all examples of eBay social networking. Other examples: MySpace, Facebook

Spoof

Email or websites made to look as though they are legitimate, but are created to deceive.

SPP

Seller Protection Policy

SPQR

Senātus Populusque Rōmānus, "The Senate and the People of Rome". Appears on Roman coins, and is used to the modern day in decoration or as insignia.

SRA *descriptive*

Self-representing Artist

S/T *descriptive*

Self-titled

Stickiness

The ability to capture and retain a visitor to a website. The more time a visitor is active on a site, the greater the opportunity for a conversion.

Sticky

Term for a web setting or preference that remains as set until changed again. Also describes website user behavior, see *Stickiness*.

Store Referral Credit

A credit applied to stores Final Value Fee when a purchaser comes to the store from outside eBay.

Stores

Special subscription service that allows sellers to offer items in a personalized area.

Stores in Search

SIS. The appearance of Stores items (SIF) in core. Notorious eBay reversal event where SIS produced dramatic sales increases, but eBay quickly removed with a number of confused statements that often appeared contradictory. Continues to play a major role in Seller push-back today.

STR

Sell-through Rate. The percent sold of product over time.

StubHub!

Stubhub.com, a website focusing on the sale of tickets to entertainment and sporting events, owned by eBay.

StumbleUpon

Stumbleupon.com, a social website focused on the discovery and sharing of interesting websites, owned by eBay.

SYI

Sell Your Item. This is the form used by Sellers to produce listings.

SZ *descriptive*

Size

T

TA

Trading Assistant. Seller that sells for others under an eBay program that establishes rules of conduct and eligibility requirements in exchange for eBay's promotion.

Take-down

A listing cancelled and removed by eBay, usually for a policy violation or under its VeRO program.

Tech Support

Customer Service that specialized in resolving technical issues.

Third Party Provider

An outside company providing services to eBay sellers

Thread

Within a discussion board (DB), an individual topic is a thread.

Thumbnail

A small graphic, usually scaled down in size, representing a larger graphic

TL

Turbo Lister. A free desktop program for making and revising listings.

TM

Trademark

TnS

Trust and Safety. Unit charged with rules enforcement and online security.

Top Line

Revenue. The income received from the sale of goods and service. NPOs use "Gross Receipts".

Town Hall

Periodic webcast presentations and Q&A with eBay executives.

Tracking

A service that allows a shipped item to be followed along major routing stops from acceptance to delivery. This is a start-to-finish system, unlike Delivery Confirmation (DC).

Tracking Number

A reference code that allows a specific item to be identified by a parcel tracking system.

Trading Assistant

TA. Seller that sells for others under an eBay program that establishes rules of conduct and eligibility requirements in exchange for eBay's promotion.

Trading Post

A business selling on consignment under the Trading Assistant program

Tranche

A subset, group, slice or subdivision of a larger set. Examples would include the $0.99 insertion fee level; Sellers with <3.9 DSRs; a Powerseller level

Transparency

A concept whereby stages of a process or activity can be readily examined. For example, being able to see a list of bidders and their bids placed as other, higher bidders became involved with an ultimate victor is a *transparent* view of the auction process.

Troll *conversational*

A person that participates in discussions with the intent to disrupt, inflame, confuse or otherwise create chaos. Trolls are not satisfied unless they get a reaction, so the recommended treatment for a troll appearance is to ignore everything it says. Lack of attention infuriates, then destroys trolls.

Trust and Safety

TnS. Unit charged with rules enforcement and online security.

T&S

Trust and Safety

Turbo Lister

TL. A free desktop program for making and revising listings.

TY *conversational*

Thank You

TYIA *conversational*

Thank You In Advance

TYVM *conversational*

Thank You Very Much

TX *conversational*

Thanks

U

UCC

Uniform Commercial Code. Uniform set of national laws that coordinate the sales of goods and transactions.

UI

See Unpaid Item.

UID

Unpaid Item Dispute

Unauthorized Use

Claim made that the use of a credit card was not authorized by the account holder as justification of a chargeback.

Uniform Commercial Code

UCC. Uniform set of national laws that coordinate the sales of goods and transactions.

Unpaid Item

UI *or* UPI. These disputes are synonymous with Non-Paying Bidder (NPB), where an item is awarded or ordered, but the buyer does not submit payment.

UPI

See Unpaid Item.

UPS

United Parcel Service

URL

Universal Resource Locator. Web address or location for something on the internet.

USPS

United States Postal Service

V

Vacation *converstaional*

Euphemism for being restricted from posting in discussion boards for getting too many "Pink Slaps." Such "vacations" may last a short while or be permanent.

VeRO

"Verified Rights Owner" is eBay's program to conform to the Digital Millennium Copyright Act (DMCA) and other issues with copyright. It is used both to refer to the program and as a verb describing a VERO action, as in "My handbags were VeRO'd by Prada and eBay removed my listings!"

VF *descriptive*

Very Fine condition

VG *or* VGC *descriptive*

Very Good Condition

VHTF *descriptive*

Very Hard To Find

Viral Marketing

A buzzword describing "word of mouth" in internet terms. With Social Networking as the vehicle for the message, it spreads at an increasingly rapid pace as more people share the message - like the spread of an infection, like a virus.

V/MC/DISC *or* V/M/D *descriptive*

Visa, Master Card, Discover

W

Want It Now

Area of eBay allowing buyers to request items they're looking to purchase, but have not found online.

Warranty Services

Service offered by eBay partner that providers extended warranty service on many new, used and refurbished products.

Web 2.0

Buzzword for internet services, sites and programs that encourage, provide or incorporate Social Networking.

Webinar

A presentation conducted on the internet.

Weblog

Blog. Self-published serial internet content, often a cross between a journal, newspaper column and a soapbox.

Webcast

A presentation or other media content that is broadcast over the internet. Q&A sessions with eBay executives, called "Town Halls", are often webcast to reach a larger audience.

WFH

Work from Home

WFHM

Work From Home Mom

Workshops

Regular presentations on various topics conducted on discussion boards.

WS *descriptive*

Widescreen. Display format for video, usually 16:9.

WTF *conversational*

The profane version of WTH

WTH *conversational*

What the hell

WYSIWYG ("whizzy-wig")

"What You See Is What You Get". Technical reference to text editors that show text as it would appear once printed or published online.

X – Y - Z

XL *descriptive*

Extra Large. Additional Xs are added to indicate the next larger size: XXL, XXXL, etc.

Year over year

Y/y. Comparison of performance.

YMMV *conversational*

Your Mileage May Vary. A euphemism for "it might be different for you."

Y/y

Year over year. Comparison of performance.

NOTES

Resources

Do You Have Suggestions?

If you have suggestions to expand the list of acronyms, terms and jargon used in this book, please email these to us at **suggestions@WordsForAuction.com**.

Write to the Authors

We love to talk to the folks in our audience, and we'd enjoy hearing from you! Please send email to us at **authors@WordsForAuction.com**

Find Even More eBay Lingo on Our Website!

Visit our website at **www.WordsForAuction.com**.

You'll also find links to the websites hosted by Danna and Uncle Joe, including:

- Internet Radio Shows
- Podcast Archives
- Helpful Articles and Resources
- eBay Classes & Internet Skills Training
- Local, Regional & National Events
- Groups, Clubs & Professional Organizations

Personal training and speaking can be arranged for your organization or event. Please contact us for details.